Fact Finders®

WORLD EXPLORERS

SIEUR DE LA SALLE

An Explorer of the Great West

by Amie Hazleton

CAPSTONE PRESS
a capstone imprint

Fact Finders Books are published by Capstone Press,
1710 Roe Crest Drive, North Mankato, Minnesota 56003
www.mycapstone.com

Library of Congress Cataloging-in-Publication Data
Names: Hazleton, Amie, author.
Title: Sieur de La Salle : an explorer of the great West / by Amie Hazleton.
Description: North Mankato, Minnesota : Capstone Press, [2016] | Series: Fact
    finders. World explorers | Includes bibliographical references and index. |
    Audience: Ages 8–12.
Identifiers: LCCN 2016025965 | ISBN 9781515742067 (library binding) | ISBN
    9781515742104 (paperback) | ISBN 9781515742524 (eBook PDF)
Subjects: LCSH: La Salle, Robert Cavelier, sieur de, 1643-1687—Juvenile literature. |
    Explorers—North America—Biography—Juvenile literature. | Explorers—
    France—Biography—Juvenile literature. | Canada—History—To 1763 (New
    France)—Juvenile literature. | Mississippi River—Discovery and exploration—
    French—Juvenile literature.
Classification: LCC F1030.5 .H39 2016 | DDC 910.92 [B]—dc23
LC record available at https://lccn.loc.gov/2016025965

Editorial Credits:
Alesha Sullivan, editor; Kayla Rossow, designer; Wanda Winch, media researcher;
Laura Manthe, production specialist

Photo Credits:
Bridgeman Images: © Look and Learn/Private Collection/James Fergus Kyle,
15, G. Dagli Orti/De Agostini Picture Library/Claude de Jongh, 7, The Stapleton
Collection/Private Collection/Arthur C. Michael, 20; Capstone, 13; Dreamstime:
Willard, cover background; Getty Images: DEA Picture Library, 11; Granger, NYC –
All rights reserved, 4, 19, 25; The Image Works: Newagen Archives, 16; North Wind
Picture Archives, cover inset, 8; Shutterstock: arigato, cardboard texture, Ensuper,
scratch paper texture, Nik Merkulov, grunge paper element, Pierre Jean Durieu, 23,
run4it, watercolor paper element, Sunny Forest, sky design element; Wikimedia:
Alanscottwalker, 27

Printed in China.
009943S17

TABLE OF CONTENTS

Introduction

La Salle's Empire

French explorer René-Robert Cavelier, Sieur de La Salle, stood at the mighty mouth of the Mississippi River in 1682. The Gulf of Mexico's blue waters stretched before him. La Salle claimed the lands whose water flowed into the Mississippi for his country. More than half of what is the present-day United States then belonged to France. La Salle named the region *Louisiana* after France's king, Louis XIV.

La Salle claimed Louisiana for France in 1682.

La Salle was the first European to explore the Mississippi from its beginning in the north all the way south at its end. Today Louisiana is a medium-sized state in the southern part of the United States. But when La Salle claimed it in 1862, Louisiana was the heartbeat and lifeline of North America. Stretching from the eastern Allegheny Mountains to the western Rockies, Louisiana was a land full of prairies, plush forests, towering mountains, and plentiful streams and rivers.

Not only did La Salle stake a huge claim of property for his homeland of France, but he also had other goals in mind. La Salle planned to set up a **colony** in Louisiana that would serve as his own **empire**. La Salle went to great lengths trying to build his empire, but his bold desire ultimately led to the explorer's disgraceful death.

colony—a territory settled by people from another country and controlled by that country

empire—a group of countries that have the same ruler

Chapter 1

THE EARLY YEARS

In 1643 René-Robert Cavelier was born in Rouen, a city in northern France. Rouen was a bustling port, filled with busy market stalls, large cathedrals, and narrow, winding streets. The Seine River snaked through the city. Ships sailed from Paris, the French capital, past Rouen, to the port of Le Havre. Some were trading ships, destined for faraway lands. Others were filled with curious **voyagers**. For Robert the ships were a daily reminder of exciting possibilities that lay across the sea.

Robert grew up in a wealthy family. His father was a trader and owned large **estates** of farmland throughout France. One estate was called La Salle. Back in the 1600s, it was common for a son to take the name of a family estate. In Robert's case, he was called Sieur de La Salle, which means "Gentleman of La Salle."

Port of Rouen in northern France

voyager—a person who takes a long journey to a distant or unknown place

estate—a large piece of property

Taking after his older brother, Jean, Robert took vows as a **novice** at the age of 17. During his six years as a novice, Robert taught at a Catholic school. As time passed Robert became restless and decided the quiet life was not for him. He gave up becoming a priest. Even though Robert had made the decision not to become a priest, he had already taken his first vows while he was a novice.

In France at the time, someone who took religious vows could not inherit family property. By law Robert could never receive his family's land. With no future in France, Robert set his sights across the Atlantic Ocean to make his fortune in the world.

Sieur de La Salle

The Ways of the Wilderness

At the age of 23, Robert boarded a ship for New France, which was France's new colony in North America. New France covered present-day eastern Canada and the Great Lakes region. La Salle was headed to meet his brother, Jean, who was already there. Jean's group of priests owned the land in Montreal, New France's capital. Montreal was located on an island in the St. Lawrence River, connecting the Great Lakes with the Atlantic Ocean. The waterfront was lined with settlers' houses that the priests provided. The priests feared attacks by local Iroquois Indians and felt these settlements would help protect them.

FACT!

Thick woods of pine and oak covered the Great Lakes region of North America. It was the homeland of the Iroquois Confederacy, an Indian nation consisting of five tribes.

novice—a person in training to become a priest

The priests gave La Salle a large piece of land at the southwest end of Montreal Island. He also had plenty of land to rent out to other settlers. La Salle cleared part of the forest in order to set up a village of his own. First he chose an area to build his own home. Then he marked off sections of land for other settlers. He charged each settler a yearly fee to live there.

La Salle quickly learned that fur trading was the best way to make a living in New France. Trading furs created a relationship between the settlers and the native peoples, who hunted and trapped animals. La Salle started studying the local Indian languages too. If he wanted to trade with them, he had to talk to them. La Salle built a trading post and grew rich from trading furs. The wealthier La Salle got, the greedier he became. He secretly hoped to eventually run the entire fur trade **enterprise** in New France.

enterprise—a unit of economic organization or activity

La Salle claimed much of the land in present-day Louisiana for his home country, France.

Early Voyages

La Salle always dreamed of the next big **expedition**. After settling on Montreal Island, he wanted to find a southwest passage, a water route that would lead to the Vermilion Sea. Today that sea is known as the Gulf of California and opens into the Pacific Ocean. La Salle knew that China was located across the Pacific Ocean. He could trade silk and other expensive goods from China and become even wealthier.

In 1669 La Salle set out by canoe to try and find the southwest passage. La Salle and his crew traveled up the St. Lawrence River and across Lake Ontario. No one is sure how far La Salle explored or what he discovered during the next two years. One by one, his men left him. La Salle's dreams of finding a southwest passage were ruined. He realized that no river flowed from the Great Lakes into the Vermilion Sea.

expedition—a long journey for a special purpose, such as exploring

Once back in Montreal, La Salle heard of a fellow explorer's voyage down the Mississippi River. In 1673 French-Canadian Louis Jolliet traveled down the "Big River," as the American Indians called it. Accompanied by Father Jacques Marquette, the two voyagers went down the Mississippi as far as the Arkansas River but did not get all the way to the river's mouth. But Jolliet was sure that the mighty Mississippi emptied into the Gulf of Mexico.

La Salle's voyages

Chapter 2

A GRIM BEGINNING

In 1677 La Salle sailed back to France to sell the king on the idea of his grand journey. King Louis liked La Salle's plan. He instructed La Salle to set up forts along the river. Now La Salle's biggest struggle was money. He needed a lot of money to pay for the trip, so La Salle borrowed some in France and in Montreal. With the money, he was able to construct the *Griffin*, a 45-ton (40-metric ton) ship equipped with five cannons. Finally in 1679 La Salle was ready to set sail from the Niagara River to the Mississippi and its mouth.

FACT!

La Salle's cannons weighed over 800 pounds (360 kilograms), were nearly 6 feet (2 meters) long, and used 4-pound (1.8-kg) iron balls as ammunition.

The *Griffin* made its way through the Great Lakes, crossing Lake Erie and Lake Huron. But on the shores of Lake Michigan, La Salle shocked his crew. The *Griffin* was a **gunboat**, meant to protect them. Instead of continuing on the journey south, La Salle loaded the *Griffin* with furs. He sent the boat back to Montreal to pay help pay off his debts. The *Griffin* was supposed to be returned to La Salle, but it was never seen again.

La Salle and his men spent nearly two years preparing for and building the *Griffin*.

gunboat—a small, fast ship with mounted guns, for use in rivers and shallow coastal waters

After the *Griffin* left for Montreal, La Salle pushed forward by canoe. Upon reaching the Illinois River, he ventured upstream and built Fort Crèvecoeur in present-day Peoria, Illinois. With winter approaching, La Salle and his men set up camp, awaiting the return of the *Griffin*. Growing impatient during the cold months, La Salle left for Montreal by canoe and on foot. The trip was more than 1,000 miles (1,610 kilometers). He set off into the wilderness with an Indian guide and four Frenchmen. It was a difficult, dangerous trip, but La Salle made it to Montreal.

La Salle and some of his men traveled by canoe for the remainder of the voyage after the *Griffin* left for France.

HENRI DE TONTY

One of La Salle's men was a daring Italian named Henri de Tonty. The two became close friends, and when La Salle left Fort Crèvecoeur to go back to Montreal, he left Tonty in charge. While La Salle was gone, his men **revolted** against Tonty and drove him off into the wilderness, alone. Upon returning to Fort Crèvecoeur, La Salle searched the waters and forests for his dear friend, but Tonty was nowhere to be found. As it happened, Tonty had been injured in an Iroquois attack and had fled to the north. After a year, La Salle finally found his old friend. Tonty was at a settlement called Michilimackinac, where Lake Michigan meets Lake Huron.

La Salle loaded another boat with supplies in Montreal and headed back to Fort Crèvecoeur. However, along the way La Salle heard word that his men at the fort had rebelled. His men were looking for him around Lake Ontario. The men felt the entire voyage was a foolish mistake. They were angry, and now they wanted La Salle dead. La Salle was furious and immediately sailed into Lake Ontario. There, he located the men and sent them back to Montreal in chains. By the fall of 1681, La Salle felt he had wasted enough time. He wanted to explore the Mississippi.

revolt—to fight against authority

Chapter 3
CLAIMING LOUISIANA

La Salle and his friend, the daring Italian Henri de Tonty, gathered a few canoes and a new crew. They entered the Illinois River in February 1682. Their crew consisted of some Frenchmen, native peoples, and a priest.

The Illinois River led them directly to the Mississippi, just north of present-day St. Louis, Missouri. They headed off toward the Gulf of Mexico. Spring was in the air as they canoed past lush trees and beautiful meadows.

Not long after, La Salle passed the mouth of the Arkansas River, which means they had gone farther than any European explorer had before. Finally, the river branched out into a wide **delta**. The mighty Mississippi was opening up to meet the Gulf of Mexico. On April 9, 1682, La Salle set his gaze on a sea of blue stretching as far as the eye could see. He had done it—he had reached the river's end.

La Salle and his crew entered the Mississippi River by canoe in 1682.

delta—a fan-shaped cluster of streams

La Salle proudly declared that Louisiana and the Mississippi belonged to his home country of France.

La Salle went ashore near present-day Venice, Louisiana, and he placed a large cross in the ground. He also placed a stone marker near the cross with King Louis's name, in honor of King Louis XIV. Then La Salle claimed the river and all the land whose water fed into it for France.

La Salle had no idea how huge this region was. Some of the longest rivers in North America flow into the great Mississippi River. For example, the Missouri River starts high in the Rocky Mountains and courses through present-day Montana, North Dakota, and South Dakota. Then the river borders Nebraska, Iowa, Kansas, and Missouri, finally crossing the state of Missouri before emptying into the Mississippi. All La Salle knew was that he had done a great service for the king of France and would be rewarded. And he could finally begin building his fur trading empire.

Chapter 4

THE DEATH OF A DREAM

Soon La Salle was back in France meeting with King Louis XIV about France's newly claimed land in Louisiana. La Salle began to argue his case for a colony. La Salle lied to the king about the exact location of the Mississippi's mouth, claiming it was much farther west than it really was.

FACT!

New Spain's capital was Mexico City, but the colony went as far north as present-day Texas, New Mexico, Arizona, and California. New Spain's great river was the Rio Grande, and it also emptied into the Gulf of Mexico.

At this time Spain owned a colony in the Americas. It was called New Spain. La Salle knew France would be in a position to fight New Spain, and the more La Salle spoke to the king, the more he lied. King Louis listened to La Salle, and his desire to take over New Spain clouded his judgment. The king agreed to establish a colony in Louisiana. King Louis XIV gave La Salle four ships, along with soldiers, craftsmen, and new settlers for the colony.

King Louis of France instructed La Salle to set up colonies in Louisiana near the mouth of the Mississippi.

On July 24, 1684, La Salle and his crew set sail from the French port of La Rochelle. Seven months later, they arrived on the Gulf Coast of Texas, at present-day Matagorda Bay. Matagorda Bay is halfway between the mouth of the Mississippi and the mouth of the Rio Grande River. La Salle told his crew that they had reached the mouth of the Mississippi—or one of its many mouths. Despite some of his French crew arguing with him, La Salle stood firm.

Things went downhill from there. The *Belle*, La Salle's supply ship, was wrecked during a storm and sank to the bottom of the bay. A second ship ran ashore and sank soon after. A third ship headed back to France.

The hot, muggy weather attracted swarms of mosquitos. Many men became weak with fever and disease and died. With no supplies, La Salle decided his only hope was to trek across the land to Canada. By this time, many of La Salle's men hated him. They were tired of La Salle's empty promises. No one wanted to go anywhere with him—and certainly not to the other side of North America.

La Salle chose 20 men for his journey, and they set out for the north. With everyone hating La Salle, the crew's anger grew day by day. By March 19, 1687, a few men came up with a plan to kill La Salle. They hid in tall grass and waited for La Salle to pass by. Then they sprang out and shot him. After La Salle's murder, his men wandered around and didn't know where to go. Only seven of them survived. Meanwhile, La Salle's body lay somewhere in Texas and has never been found. La Salle's dream of a Louisiana fur empire would never come true.

La Salle landed on the Gulf of Mexico in 1685.

FACT!

In 1995, the *Belle* was discovered at the bottom of Matagorda Bay, Texas.

In the years to come, France and Britain were often at war. Their fighting trickled over into their colonies in North America. By 1760 Britain had won all of Canada and the French settlements near the Great Lakes. In 1763 Britain took control of all French territory east of the Mississippi.

The history of New France came to an end in 1803. That year the United States bought the Louisiana territory from France for $15 million. This **transaction** is known as the Louisiana Purchase. The Louisiana territory stretched from the Rocky Mountains east to the Mississippi River. The Louisiana Purchase doubled the size of the United States.

LOYAL TO THE END

La Salle had a couple of his men remain faithful to him to the end. One man was Henri Joutel, a man from La Salle's hometown. Joutel described La Salle as possessing many "fine qualities" but also said he had a "haughtiness . . . and a harshness towards those under his command." Joutel's claims could have been the cause of La Salle's murder, as his men started to hate him. Henri de Tonty, however, was La Salle's dear friend through it all. Tonty called the explorer "one of the greatest men of his age."

A statue of La Salle in Lincoln Park in Chicago

transaction—an exchange of goods, services, or money

Timeline

1643: René-Robert Cavelier, Sieur de La Salle is born in Rouen, France

1660: La Salle takes vows as a novice, in hopes of becoming a priest

1666: La Salle sails to New France, which is France's new colony in North America

1669–1671: In search of the southwest passage, La Salle explores the Great Lakes and the Midwest

1679: La Salle and his crew sail the *Griffin* through the Great Lakes to Illinois

1682: La Salle explores the Mississippi River south to the Gulf of Mexico and claims the Mississippi River Valley for France, including Louisiana

1684: La Salle has King Louis XIV's approval to start a settlement near the mouth of the Mississippi

1685: La Salle and his crew arrive at present-day Matagorda Bay, Texas

1687: La Salle is killed by his own men in Texas, and his body is never found

1803: The history of New France comes to an end, as the U.S. purchases Louisiana from France, known as the Louisiana Purchase

Important People

Louis de Frontenac (1622–1698)—governor of New France

Louis Jolliet (1645–1700)—French-Canadian who explored the upper Mississippi River with Father Jacques Marquette in 1673

Louis XIV (1638–1715)—king of France, called the Sun King

Jacques Marquette (1637–1675)—priest who explored the upper Mississippi River with Louis Jolliet in 1673

Henri de Tonty (1650?–1704)—Italian-born explorer who joined La Salle on his explorations

GLOSSARY

colony (KOL-uh-nee)—a territory settled by people from another country and controlled by that country

delta (DEL-tuh)—a fan-shaped cluster of streams

empire (EM-pire)—a group of countries that have the same ruler

enterprise (ENT-uhr-prize)—a unit of economic organization or activity

estate (ess-TATE)—a large piece of property

expedition (ek-spuh-DISH-uhn)—a long journey for a special purpose, such as exploring

gunboat (GUHN-boht)—a small, fast ship with mounted guns, for use in rivers and shallow coastal waters

novice (NOV-iss)—a person in training to become a priest

revolt (ri-VOHLT)—to fight against authority

transaction (tran-ZAK-shuhn)—an exchange of goods, services, or money

voyager (VOY-uh-jer)—a person who takes a long journey to a distant or unknown place

READ MORE

Kuligowski, Stephanie. *La Salle: Early Texas Explorer.* Primary Source Readers: Texas History. Huntington Beach, Calif.: Teacher Created Materials, 2012.

O'Brien, Cynthia. *Explore with Sieur de La Salle.* Travel with the Great Explorer. New York: Crabtree Publishing, 2015.

Raum, Elizabeth. *Expanding a Nation: Causes and Effects of the Louisiana Purchase.* Cause and Effect. North Mankato, Minn.: Capstone Press, 2014.

INTERNET SITES

FactHound offers a safe, fun way to find Internet sites related to this book. All of the sites on FactHound have been researched by our staff.

Here's all you do:

Visit *www.facthound.com*

Type in this code: 9781515742067

Super-cool stuff!

Check out projects, games and lots more at
www.capstonekids.com

CRITICAL THINKING USING THE COMMON CORE

1. How did Sieur de La Salle's childhood influence his decision to sail across the Atlantic Ocean to New France? (Integration of Knowledge and Ideas)

2. Why did La Salle want to build a fur trading enterprise in New France? (Key Ideas and Details)

3. Do you think La Salle's voyages were a success or failure for France? Why? (Integration of Knowledge and Ideas)

INDEX

31901064821996